faith stories for today

Angela Wood

BBC
Longman

This book is full of my favourite kind of stories – the kind that go back a long way and have been told by different people at different times and in different places. When bits from the life of the storyteller and the listeners creep in, the story really *works*. It can happen for us today, too, because these deep, changing stories are about *being human*, whenever you live, whatever you look like, wherever you are. . .and *we are* human, aren't we? (Well, I am!)

Another thing I like about this kind of story is that it reminds me of a sweet – one you can suck for ages and even when it's all gone, you can still taste it. Sometimes I have a little puzzle in my mind about life but when I read or tell the stories, I end up with more questions than I started with! (That might happen to you – so don't say you haven't been warned!) Then I remember that these faith stories are for asking questions, not really for telling answers. My pet name for them is '*Why?* stories'.

Some people helped me with this book by saying what they thought when I told, read or showed them these stories. So I would like to thank Zaki Badawi, Hugo Gryn, Kanwaljit Kaur, Mathoor Krishnamurti, Indarjit Singh and the wonderful children of Lampton, Springwell Junior and Wellington Schools. But most of all I would like to thank Ester Gluck who is 'zany' as well as 'sensitive'.

My father died when I was nine. This book helps me to remember him because he taught me to question everything and told me stories for the asking.

Contents

A dream of a place	*Jewish*	4
Inside out	*Muslim*	10
Growing up	*Christian*	16
A world of his own	*Sikh*	22
Taking sides	*Sikh*	28
Just a drop	*Jewish*	34
What it's worth	*Muslim*	40
Something in the air	*Hindu*	46
All together	*Hindu*	52
Cup final	*Christian*	58

A dream *of* a place

Solomon was one of those people who paid a lot of attention to their dreams and every morning he went through in his mind what had happened in his sleep. Often his dreams made no sense to him at all and he would ask other people what they meant.

Although King Solomon was supposed to be wise, there were actually many choices he found hard to make. What was bothering him was where to build the Temple. Obviously it had to be somewhere that everybody could get to easily. It

had to be in beautiful surroundings. . .but there was something else. The place itself had to say something about what the Temple was for, what the whole idea was of worshipping God. One morning, Solomon leapt out of bed and knew the exact spot. . .

On the top of Mount Moriah, there was a field owned by two brothers. They got on well and worked hard to make things grow. If they had any problems, they talked them over, and they always made decisions together. 'What shall we plant this year?' they'd say and they'd sort it out. Whenever they had to buy something for their field, they paid half each and at the end of the harvest they divided the crops evenly.

The only difference between them was the way they lived. One of them had a house in a corner of the field where he lived on his own with just a few animals. His brother was married, had several children ranging from babies to teenagers, and they lived in the house in the opposite corner of the field.

One evening, the single brother wondered, 'Why do my brother and I get the same? He has several mouths to feed but there's only one of me! I know, in the morning I'll take him some of the crops from my barn. . .oh, but he'll never accept them. I can just hear him saying, "Fair's fair! We put the same in. We take the same out." I'll have to get it to him when he's not looking. As soon as it's dark, I'll fill a sack in my barn, trudge across the field and over the hill to *his* barn. Then I'll empty it into his granary and slip quietly back across the field. He'll never know how it got there and he'll have a lovely surprise.'

Many Jewish stories that look for meanings are **midrashim**. A midrash is a story which tries to answer people's questions about life in general or about just one thing.

About 2000 years ago, when some Jews were wondering why their Temple was built in a particular place, this midrash was told.

At exactly the same moment, the married brother wondered, 'Why do my brother and I get the same? I have a wonderful family. My wife and I care for our children while they are young and we know they will care for us when we are old. But my brother lives all alone. I wonder if he is lonely. I know, in the morning I'll take him some of the crops from my barn . . . oh, but he'll never accept them. I can just hear him saying, "Fair's fair! We put the same in. We take the same out." I'll have to get it to him when he's not looking. As soon as it's dark, I'll fill a sack in my barn, trudge across the field and over the hill to *his* barn. Then I'll empty it into his granary and slip quietly back across the field. He'll never know how it got there and he'll have a lovely surprise.'

Did you have any idea that the two brothers would do the same for each other? What did you think would happen *in the end*?

Why do people sometimes want a special place for worship? What made the place that Solomon chose so special? What *else* could happen in a place to make it be remembered as somewhere special for worship?

At dead of night, each brother set out for the opposite corner, with a heavy sack on his back. Each crept into his brother's barn, laid down his gift, silently closed the door behind him and hurried back in secret.

But when they returned to their own barn, each brother found a sack still there. Utterly mystified, he loaded up once more and began the journey back to his brother's store. Again and again, there was always one more sack.

Up and down, back and forth they went, bearing loads of love through the night.

As dawn broke, the two brothers crossed on the top of the hill and saw each other face to face. Realising what had happened, they started to laugh. Then their hearts filled up, tears flowed down their cheeks, and they hugged and danced till morning.

Inside out

'He's gone! He's gone!' shrieked Fari, jumping up and down, her nose twitching in excitement.

'Sh! What if he hasn't. . .?' Imfar squeaked. But as they spoke, they saw through a crack in the wall the familiar shape of Simsim – the neighbourhood cat, their most determined persecutor. He was climbing into a taxi, while the driver strapped the luggage onto the roof-rack and slammed the door. 'The airport, please!' the cat miaowed, adding with importance, 'Saudi Arabian check-in! And *please* hurry: I simply *must* be on the flight to Jedda!'

The cab sped off down the road and the mice leapt for joy. 'When the cat's away, mice will play!' Asfar reminded them all. 'And are *we* going to play!' Edfar tooted her flute, Olfar beat his drum; they all joined hands in a circle and danced so fast that the mouse-hole itself started to rock. Soon Urfar appeared with plates of nibbles – crunchy nuts, dried fruit and ripe cheese. Their tiny feet were blistered from dancing and their jaws ached from laughing, but they were contented little mice who flopped onto cushions and fell into a deep sleep.

By the time they woke up, Simsim was landing at Jedda. It had been a smooth, comfortable flight and already he had got to know some of his fellow pilgrims. It was the time of the year when Muslims from all over the world make this journey to the Ka'aba – the first altar to Allah – and the place where the Prophet Muhammad was born. It was around Makka that Allah had given the Prophet so many ideas for the world, so going there was getting in touch with all of that inside you.

Not every Muslim would be there *this* year but they all felt they should make the trip at least once in their life, if they could. For most of them, it would be a one-off and that was partly why Simsim was so nervous. 'As a cat I may have nine lives,' he reminded himself, stroking his whiskers, 'but this is my first and probably last hajj: I want to get things right first time. I probably won't have another chance!'

On the plane, Simsim had trimmed his claws, washed as he did before praying and put on the special long white cloth that he had brought with him. He wrapped it round his waist, tucked it in and threw the rest of it over his shoulder. The other hajjis had done that, too, and they all looked the same, wearing their ihram. 'That's how it should be!' mused Simsim. 'Allah doesn't care who's a Cool Cat or who's a Top Dog!'

Makka was a tail's length away from Jedda and hajjis kept calling out, 'Here I come!' getting louder and faster as they got closer to the city. Simsim had never ridden a camel before and it was fun to whizz past the donkeys, buses and people on foot. At times, he wished *he* had travelled by paw as the camel ride made the fur on his neck stand on end!

His guide in Makka had a bowl of cool, creamy milk waiting for him and greeted him, 'Assalamu aleikum!' Simsim touched his paw to his chest and replied, 'Wa aleikum salam!' Then the two of them went to hunt for the hotel.

The Ka'aba was beyond Simsim's wildest dreams. As the swirling crowds encircled the ancient stone, pressing forward to kiss it, Simsim felt every one of his whiskers tingling...

At Zamzam, there is a special spring and even before

he could see or hear it, Simsim's tail began to quiver. The cheetah in him surged forth and he raced to the fresh water, outpacing the two-legged pilgrims.

All the hajjis were on Mount Arafat together and when they prayed silently, there wasn't a miaow to be heard for miles. 'A most welcome paws for thought!' Simsim chuckled. Tents went up all over the plain and a delicious smell of cooking wafted on the breeze. They served Simsim fish just the way he liked it – raw and with the head left on.

The next stop was Mina and Simsim was already dreading having his head shaved. 'I know I'm supposed to be a baby,

starting life again after hajj,' he thought, 'but kittens aren't born *bald*! And anyway, I've become very attached to my fur – or rather, my fur has become very attached to me!' Going round the Ka'aba again, Simsim's ears stuck out and he felt a bit funny. He also felt funny leaving Makka: it had really been the experience of a lifetime and he felt a completely new cat.

The mice were lazing in the sun when Simsim's taxi turned the corner. 'D-rat!' they screeched and scuttled under floorboards for safety. Gradually, a few of the brave ventured out to explore and they caught a glimpse of something rare and wonderful: the transformation of Simsim! He had brought

souvenirs of the hajj and special Muslim items from Makka and Mina. On a shelf was a model of the Ka'aba and decorative metal plaques showing the names of Allah in Arabic. On the big wall, in blue and green, hung a magnificent embroidered hanging, depicting the Prophet's mosque in Medina. But what really made them gasp was the sight of Simsim himself, their arch-enemy, sitting cross-legged on his prayer mat, engrossed in reading the Qur'an from its stand. Wearing a prayer cap, he fingered beads of precious Tiger's Eye stones – one for each of the 99 names of Allah. 'That's some cat!' Farel exclaimed and scuttled back to tell the others.

'Many Muslims say that the hajj is the most important event of their life and really changes them deep down,' explained Faron, 'though how it happens is very complicated...well, complicatted, anyway! Perhaps we could shake tails and be friends. There is a very "mice" custom of going to congratulate and welcome a hajji. Nefar, will you go on our behalf?'

'Not me! I know that cat too well!'

'What are you – a mouse or a man?'

'I'm alive and I'd like to keep it that way!'

'All right, who then?'

'Fara! Fara!' a group volunteered. 'She's good at that sort of thing!' They all agreed – all except Fara. Her frail body trembled and her tiny teeth chattered as they nudged her to the front. 'You could charm the birds off the trees!' Nefar remarked. 'And Simsim would adore that! There was a chorus of laughter and mousy smiles all round.

When Fara reached Simsim's room, he was in the same

position – absolutely still, with his eyes closed. 'Let sleeping cats lie!' she thought to herself, tiptoeing reluctantly across the carpet. Simsim did not budge. 'Hmhm! Hmhm!' she coughed to attract his attention, sidling a little closer. 'Assa. . .Assalamu,' she stuttered. 'Assalamu aleikum!'

Simsim opened one eye, took one look at the tasty dinner in front of him and drew himself up to his full size. The petrified mouse recoiled in fright, backed into the Qur'an stand a split second before the huge creature pounced. A second time he struck, but missed her again as she dodged behind the desk, her tiny heart pounding in her chest. She cowered there for a moment, trying to calm down and think clearly. 'What am I doing here?' she wondered. 'How could I be so stupid?' Before she could answer herself, she saw the monster's claws coming towards her and she knew she was on the run again. Scuttling along the wall, she spied a hole in the corner and dived in, the tip of her tail escaping the clutches of the feline foe by a hair's breadth. Fara heard him scream, 'Rats!' as she scampered along the narrow passageway, took a flying leap and landed breathless in the nest.

'He *prays* like a hajji,' she panted, 'but *hunts* like a cat!'

There is a Syrian folktale about a cat who went to Makka. It is about not judging other people and about being sincere yourself. 'Far' is Arabic for 'mouse'. In this version, the names of all the mice have 'far' in them. 'Simsim' means 'sesame' and it is a pet name for a cat.

Was Simsim really a cat on the inside and a hajji on the outside? or a hajji on the inside and a cat on the outside?

Is it important for people to be the same inside and out? If so, how?

Growing up

Leaves rustled, mud squelched and twigs snapped. The three gardeners looked up, downed tools and scratched their heads as the Superintendent of Parks made an entrance through the shrubbery. Why couldn't their boss come along the paths like anyone else?

Common-or-garden Superpark had something important to say. 'I have to go to a meeting and I'll be off-site for some time. Can I rely on you to keep things going – or, should I say, growing?'

'Great!' thought Green Fingers. 'Here's a real chance to prove what I can do.'

'It'll be nice not to have to worry about work too much!' was Grow Bag's first reaction. 'I'm sick of all this raking and hoeing. I want to enjoy life!'

For Flower Pot, it was a totally different story. 'I don't know if I can cope without Superpark around. I haven't got a clue about this work. I'm told what to do and I get on with it.'

'The thing is,' Superpark continued, 'this park can't be allowed to turn into a wilderness just because I'm not here and I do *not* expect to come back and find everything's gone to seed, eh? Joke!'

Grow Bag, Green Fingers and Flower Pot exchanged glances and attempted a feeble laugh.

'I've got some rather special varieties of seed here and I'm trusting you to take good care of them.' The three gardeners heard the familiar sound of dry seeds as Superpark handed out the little paper packets. They were attracted by the brightly coloured pictures and squinted to read the small print. Their concentration was broken by a rustle of leaves and they caught the last glimpse of Superpark disappearing through the hedge.

Clutching the packets firmly, Flower Pot made straight for the shed where there was a wooden box on the top shelf.
'I don't want these getting damaged or stolen so I'll keep them under lock and key, and bolt the potting-shed door.'

Grow Bag figured out, 'If I get these into the ground quickly, I can leg it over to the swings and slides and have a bit of fun before the park closes.' It really didn't take much time at all to scatter the seeds on the soil, sprinkle some moss peat and turn on the hose.

By then, Green Fingers was on the way back from the library with a book on how to look after delicate plants. It explained how important it is to be patient and gentle with young seedlings. It said that plants are like people because they both need tender loving care and that a good gardener believes deep down that something really wonderful can begin with a tiny speck.

Jesus told many parables to help people understand things in life which are difficult or complicated. A parable is usually about something quite ordinary and familiar. Sometimes the storyteller explains *how* the complicated thing is like the ordinary thing; but sometimes the storyteller leaves it to the listeners to work out for themselves!

This story is adapted from the 'parable of the talents' which is recorded in the Bible (Matthew 25 and Luke 19). A 'talent' was a sum of money and we get the word for someone's ability from this story. But this modern version has seeds instead of talents.

Every day, on the way to the skate ramps or the adventure playground, Grow Bag would enjoy seeing a few shoots gradually turning into fully-fledged plants and would help them along by pulling out a weed or two.

People strolling through the grounds always stopped to admire Green Fingers' glorious plantations where all sorts of life were flourishing. Green Fingers tended it almost day and night – weeding and watering, fertilising and fussing...

And all the while, Flower Pot stood guard outside the shed to keep off vandals.

The three gardeners had almost forgotten about Superpark until the day they saw the hedge moving again...

'I've still got your seeds!' exclaimed Flower Pot. 'Nothing's happened to them since you gave them to me.'

Superpark didn't need to be shown what Grow Bag and Green Fingers had done .....

Did Grow Bag really care for the seeds more than Flower Pot? Should Green Fingers have *not* worked so hard on the seeds and perhaps spent more time with the family or enjoying hobbies? Was Common-or-garden Superpark fair to the gardeners in the end?

What is the complicated idea that the park and the gardeners are like? What do you think the parable is really about?

'One of the things decided at the meeting was the need for our parks and gardens to grow. You've got a few nice things going there, Grow Bag, and I'd like to put you in charge of our allotment project. What do you say?' Grow Bag nodded vigorously.

'Green Fingers, this is too beautiful for words. Would you take on responsibility for new developments?' They shook hands.

Flower Pot stood waiting, too choked to speak, with a sad but hopeful expression. 'Don't worry, Flower Pot. You've still got your job here and I know what you're thinking,' said Superpark. 'You've kept the seeds safe and dry but I asked you to *care* for them. Seeds aren't meant to *stay* seeds. They're supposed to fill the world with flowers and fruit, with beautiful colours and delicious scents. All you've done is stop them growing.'

A world *of* his own

'You're too hard on the boy, dear!' said Mata Tripta, softly reproaching her husband. 'He's only a child: why can't you let him be himself?'

'Don't you remember when he was born?' – her face lit up with the memory – 'and you asked Pandit Hardial for his horoscope? And when he saw the baby he immediately bowed – I'll never forget it – and touched his feet. Have you forgotten what the astrologer said about our Nanak?'

He shook his head and she egged him on gently to say it. 'He said he could tell we had a very unusual son who will be loved and respected by *everyone*. He'll become rich, famous and successful and even rise to great power...'

'There! And you must admit, he *was* a beautiful baby: he almost never cried; he just lay in his crib and smiled at the sky, his eyes sparkling like the stars. Do babies *think*, I wonder. It may seem funny, but I'm sure Nanak was a thinker even then.'

'A daydreamer more like!' Baba Kalu retorted. 'Imagine what he's like at school! Probably got his head in the clouds all day – I really pity his poor teacher!'

Nanak's father was interrupted by the sound of voices outside and he ran to the window. Seeing Nanak with his teacher in the street, his curiosity turned to shock and he turned away quickly. 'It's Pandit Gopal, bringing Nanak home early. I bet he's decided that he probably can't teach him a thing because he never concentrates and now he's getting expelled!'

'Forgive me for coming like this,' the teacher began, 'but I just had to tell you what an extraordinary child you have. Whatever it is, he gets the hang of it in no time at all. When he first came to us and I taught the class the Hindi alphabet, you would have thought he already knew it – incredible! In fact, he teaches me more than I teach him.' Baba Kalu's mouth dropped open in amazement; but Mata Tripta glowed.

'Today,' Pandit Gopal went on, 'I noticed he was sitting on his own, humming a tune I'd never heard before and engrossed in something he was writing. When I read it, I instinctively touched it to my head. It had a very special quality. It was all about nature and God, about how God loves the whole world – people, animals and everything – and how beautiful life can be if we care enough. It was an acrostic, you know, a poem where the first letters of each line spell out the alphabet in the right order, going down. It's ever so hard. I believe your boy may actually be God in a human body, come to our life to show us goodness.' And he bowed to Guru Nanak.

Their son. . .an avatar? It was the most ridiculous thing Baba Kalu had ever heard but Mata Tripta just smiled.

Guru Nanak's parents agreed there was no point in him going back to Pandit Gopal's class if there was nothing he could teach him. So for several years he learnt poetry and scripture from religious leaders which he enjoyed thoroughly.

'It's not right,' exclaimed Baba Kalu, 'for someone to read and think all day. A young man his age should be doing something useful by now. He's got no qualifications – nothing to show for himself. He ought to have a proper job and be bringing in some money!'

At last it was decided that Guru Nanak would be put to work herding cattle. Baba Kalu was pleased because it was something *practical* and Guru Nanak had the chance of a quiet life in the open air – a perfect solution.

It worked quite well for a while: Guru Nanak would take the cattle out to graze and the cows, calves and buffaloes followed him as if he had *always* been their herdsman. Together, they wandered through the village and along the paths to the pasture. Guru Nanak spotted brightly coloured birds flitting in and out of the woods. He saw trees, once rich with green leaves from the monsoon rain, burst into blossom in the spring sunshine. He listened to the murmur of bees and the shrill cries of peacocks. What a wonderful world it was!

But it was bound to happen sooner or later. It was a particularly warm day and Guru Nanak sat under a tree and lost himself in thought. Why, he wondered, did the sun rise and set? Who made the moon and stars? What were we born for? What happens when we die? Why are we all different? What makes people nasty? Why could life be so unfair?

It is hard to say how long he had been there, silently mulling over these questions and drinking in the glorious atmosphere. . .when suddenly his peace of mind was shattered by angry shouts and wild gestures. Pulling himself up and raising his hand to his brow to shield his eyes from the sun, Guru Nanak stared hard into the middle distance – and cringed.

The cattle he was responsible for had wandered through the hedge to munch some fresh green corn which the farmer had been cultivating in the next field. In their enthusiasm for such a succulent feast, they had trampled on the tender stalks and spoiled the crop. 'Ooh! No wonder he's so angry,' thought Guru Nanak.

'Hey-up! Shoo!' shouted the farmer at the startled cattle, brandishing a stick for emphasis. As he rushed towards them, Guru Nanak could see the fury on his face. But the louder he yelled and the harder he thrust with his stick, the more frantic the cows became until they were rampaging all over the young corn in wild abandon. By the time the distraught man had driven the last animal back through the hedge, his farm was flattened and his livelihood utterly ruined. He stood there, beating the air with his stick, his eyebrows knit together in rage. 'I'll get you!' he hollered as the concerned young man came towards him. 'You'll pay for this!'

He expected Guru Nanak to say he was sorry, that he had fallen asleep in the sun; or even make out that it wasn't his fault, that cows will be cows... So he was quite dumbfounded at the Guru's reaction: 'Please don't be cross! If you wait, God will bless your land and it will yield more than ever.' The disgruntled corn-grower was hardly convinced. 'What kind of compensation is that?' he demanded to know. 'If that's all you can offer, I'm going to Rai Bular to lodge a complaint.'

Guru Nanak looked with love and pity on the demolished plot, then closed his eyes...

By the time he reached Rai Bular's house, all the veins on the farmer's forehead were standing up and his jaw was tight with anger. A crowd instantly gathered, keen to be in the know on local affairs. 'But Nanak *always* sits and thinks,' a woman explained. 'When he was younger, he was asleep once under a tree and a snake slithered up to him. It rose up over his face and could easily have killed him with a single bite but instead it puffed up its hood to shade him from the sun, and it stayed all day, protecting him from the heat.'

That jogged the memory of one of her neighbours. 'Once he sat under some branches but if the sun had moved across the sky during the day, the tree would not have been able to save him from getting burnt. So the sun stayed still all day!'

'What's all this?' asked Rai Bular, coming out of his house, and when he was told why the landowner was so aggrieved, he judged immediately that he must be repaid in full.

'But please, at least look at it,' Guru Nanak requested. 'I'm sure it's all right and there's no need to get upset!'

'Is he calling me a liar?'

'No, but I am saying in front of everyone what I said to you on your own: God will bless your land.'

So Rai Bular sent two people to go to the site with the owner to assess the damage. Before they got there, they stopped dead in their tracks: not a blade of grass was broken, not a head of corn was eaten and the tender plants waved gently in the evening breeze.

Guru Nanak became the first of the ten Sikh gurus (teachers). Born into a Hindu family in India, about 400 years ago, he questioned his own religious upbringing and believed that everyone should be able to think for themselves.

How can you explain what happened to the field of corn? Did Guru Nanak have power to change it back? Did God do it to make what Guru Nanak said come true? How could you tell if someone had special powers? Would it show when they were a baby? at school?

Do you ever wonder about the same things as Guru Nanak? Have you ever come up with any answers to those questions? What else do you wonder about?

Taking sides

Thwack! Crunch! Boff! Zap! Aaah!

Fighting had been very fierce for several weeks and from early morning the two sides had been giving each other a particularly serious hammering. Glares were exchanged, with menacing eyes and bared teeth, as the warriors engaged in the most desperate struggle of their lives – a fight to the finish... Winning was everything!

The sun beat down mercilessly, sweat poured off the soldiers' brows and their bodies flagged with exhaustion. By evening, the battlefield was strewn with the defeated and the dying. The corpses and the collapsed lay side by side, overlapping or even heaped together on the ground. The air was filled with the stench of blood and the mingled cries of pain.

As dusk fell, a lone figure was silhouetted against the sky, treading carefully, and weaving in and out of the piles of bodies. On a thick strap around Khaneeya's neck was slung a huge leather bottle and as he passed each soldier he called out, 'Water! Water! Who needs water?' Some of the injured could barely raise an eyebrow. Some could only manage a limp wave of the hand or a tired, aching moan.

At every sign of life, Khaneeya poured a few precious drops into the mouths of the wounded. Many of them revived and his cheerful, loving words brought them hope.

But Khaneeya's actions were spotted by his comrades in the Sikh army. 'Hey, Khaneeya!' they yelled, 'What do you think you're doing?' He pretended not to hear. 'Oi! You're quenching their blokes' thirst not just our lot... Have you gone over to the other side or can't you tell the difference?'

'I know who's who, all right,' replied Khaneeya, carrying on.

'Look, Khaneeya,' said one of the bigger men, 'if you don't stop helping the other lot...!'

One of the other Sikhs put a hand on his shoulder. 'Don't mess with that bloke. I reckon Guru Gobind Singh should work it all out. He's chief around here.' They all agreed.

'My saint-soldiers,' said Guru Gobind Singh in a warm, gentle voice, 'the battle is over for the day but you look ready to kill!'

Sikhs love to tell stories from the lives of the ten gurus, the teachers of their tradition. About 300 years ago, the last human guru, Guru Gobind Singh created the khalsa, the Sikh community. The guru who came after him and did not die was the Sikh scripture, the *Guru Granth Sahib*.

'He's a traitor! Or else he's gone mad! He's dishing out water to Sikhs who have fainted *and* to "them". We slog our guts out all day, knocking them out, and he gets them going again so they can do us in tomorrow! What are you going to do about him?'

The guru was not the kind of person who jumped to conclusions. 'I'm not going to "do" anything about him,' he replied. 'I think I'll stroll over and have a little chat.' He was not called 'true king' for nothing.

'There is a rumour, Khaneeya, that you have been helping our enemies. What do you have to say for yourself?'

'It's not true!'

'Look at me: are you telling me that you have *not* been helping the enemy?'

'I don't *have* any enemies... I see looks of pain, I hear cries of agony and I feel they're just people, children of the same God who made me. *They* need water, too.'

'Oh, Khaneeya,' said Guru Gobind Singh, hugging him tightly, his eyes filling with tears. 'What a super person you are! A really terrific Sikh! We're fighting this war to hang on to our faith and our faith tells us everyone is equal, with a right to life and the freedom to find God in their own way. What you did was really marvellous because you showed that feeling was maybe more important than actually winning the war.

How do you imagine that Guru Gobind Singh 'handled' the others? What might he have said to them to make them believe Bhai Khaneeya was doing the best thing?

Is it right for a group of people to fight to defend their religion if another group is attacking it? Or should someone who is religious never fight at all?

'When you go back, take this from me,' and he handed him ointment and bandages. 'I want to call you "Bhai" because you are a real brother . . .'

Bhai Khaneeya thanked the guru, 'But what about the rumour?'

'Don't worry about the others!' Guru Gobind Singh grinned. 'I can handle them!'

As Bhai Khaneeya headed back to the battlefield, Guru Gobind Singh summoned the rest of his men. 'When an army is attacking us and our religion, they are enemies but once they lie wounded they are just humans, I would even say, our friends.'

His eyes scanned the plain and there was Bhai Khaneeya kneeling down to a man from the other side to dress his wounds.

Just *a* drop

'You worry too much, Shuvi. It's dead simple. All we had to do was find our favourite thing,' Feleh explained.

'No – we had to get the most *precious* thing in all the world,' Shuvi corrected him.

'Same difference!'

'Yeah? Why did we have to do it, anyway?'

'Search me. I'm not God, am I?' replied Feleh, sounding obvious.

'The thing is,' interrupted Zedka, 'we've all brought something, so let's take a look. Bags be first!' Out of her backpack she pulled a small square of white cloth with a red mark in the middle. She opened it out on her lap and smoothed it down.

'Strawberry jam – yummy!' guessed Shuvi.

'Ha! ha!' came a sarcastic laugh.

'Tomato sauce. . .' suggested Feleh. 'You had some lovely chips and got ketchup all over your hanky!'

'Oh, honestly! It's blood!'

'Me next!' piped Feleh. Taking care to keep it upright, he brought out of his satchel a test tube which he held firmly between his thumb and forefinger. It contained a small amount of yellow fluid and had a cork stopper.

'Is it from some scientific experiment?' Zedka wondered.

'No, but you're close.'

'Ooh, I know,' cried Shuvi. 'It's a magic potion!'

But Feleh dismissed her idea with a wave of the hand. 'It's a shot of vaccine!'

Shuvi had had to keep her lunchbox absolutely level and carry it very steadily. She took out a minute, round dish, placed it gently on her palm and held out her hand flat. The other two stared at it for a moment, barely making out that there was something clear in the bottom.

'Don't tell me you've been catching rain!' enquired Feleh cheekily.

'Or stealing holy water!' Zedka accused jokingly.

'Not at all! It's a tear!'

The three of them sat back and pondered their various finds: it was strange they had all chosen small drops of something; even stranger that they had been unable to guess what each other's choice was; and strangest of all that no one else could imagine *why* they'd chosen that particular treasure.

Had they come up with the things that were actually precious to God, they needed to know? How could they find out? Maybe God had let them be free to decide for themselves and would say that whatever they chose – and really meant – was right... Did it matter that they were different? Can you logically have more than one *most* precious thing? Why had God sent them off to find the most valuable thing of all? Surely God already knew the answer... So what was this game all about? What would anyone get out of it? And what, in the end, would God make of their funny little efforts?

Round and round they went, turning so many questions over in their mind. 'Maybe there are some things about God that we'll never understand,' Shuvi reflected after a while.

But Feleh spoke for all three of them when he exclaimed, 'I've got brain pain!'

'Why don't we just come out with it and tell each other *why* we collected the drops?' said Zedka, trying to be practical. 'Who knows, perhaps we've all hit on the same idea. If we haven't, maybe we could vote on the one most precious thing out of all our precious three...'

They nodded in agreement and leaned back to show she could go first. Zedka spread out her blood-stained piece of gauze and began her tale. 'In a South American village, high up in the mountains, the life of the peasants is a bitter struggle. They are downtrodden by wealthy landowners who charge them high rents and take a greedy share of the crops they grow. Foreign businessmen make them work long hours for low wages in dangerous mines or dirty factories. "Enough of this!" declared a young man one day. He was the eldest son in his family. "Our government is full of crooks. They steal from the poor to give to the rich. Wherever we turn for help, the door is slammed in our face! There has to be a better life!"

' "There is, my boy," his mother replied. "It is beyond the grave. We have been told our reward will be in heaven."

' "They only tell us that to keep us quiet, to stop us complaining! It's no good, Mama! There are other young men who think like me. We're going to fight. We'll change it all, you'll see!" Putting on his soldier's cap, he kissed his mother goodbye and ran down the mountainside, brave and free. The next she saw of him was when a donkey came clip-clop up the hill, bringing his body home. "Sweet Mama..." he called softly before he died.

'And here,' Zedka announced, 'is his final drop of blood – the most precious thing in all the world.'

Gripping the test tube between thumb and forefinger, Feleh cleared his throat and described his scene. 'In Central Africa there was a clinic – the only one for hundreds of miles – which was run single-handed by a devoted nurse. Though conditions were hard and resources scarce, no one in need of her help was ever turned away and she worked tirelessly, coaxing her patients back to health or bringing comfort to the dying. Not once did she complain of the hardship and not once did she have a selfish thought. Whenever she was asked how long she had been at the clinic, she would smile and say sweetly, "This is my life!"

'One day an epidemic struck the whole area. Entire families died from the disease and her clinic soon became overcrowded. Day and night, she nursed her patients, often tired and weak herself. She offered them water and mopped their fevered brows, saving the little vaccine there was for the babies and children. Before long, she too was in the grip of the same sickness and she collapsed in the corner of the ward. All night, as the fever raged in her infected body, she fought for her life but in the morning, with a prayer on her lips, she died. And here,' Feleh announced, 'is the vaccine that could have saved her – the most precious thing in all the world.'

Finally, Shuvi placed the dish gently on the flat of her hand and told her story. 'There was a well-known thief in Eastern Europe. Not trusting anyone, he worked alone and at night. Everyone knew he was a burglar but could never prove it as he was too good at his job.

'All his adult life, he had never known anything but crime: he had snatched handbags, picked pockets, robbed banks, forged cheques and held up trains.

'And then, one snowy night, he went out on a job. There was a house he had had his eye on for some time. Covering his tracks, he crept into the yard and down the alley at the side. He could drop in through a window without being noticed. A drainpipe was perfectly placed and he scaled it in no time, but just then he heard sounds coming from inside. Edging his way from one sill to the next, he peered through a gap in the curtains into a room full of happiness: the grandmother was knitting and the grandfather was singing at the piano; children played together on the rug; the father was piling logs onto the fire and in an armchair the mother was feeding her baby. Their closeness and contentment touched him deeply and there was a look on their faces and a sound in their voices that reminded him of his own family he had loved so dearly when he was a boy and the good, simple life he had left behind.

'Filled with regret, he turned away and jumped back into the yard. Overcome with shame, he crouched down and wept. And here,' Shuvi announced, 'is a single tear of a soul that is truly sorry – the most precious thing in all the world.'

This is based on a Jewish folktale which is often told around Yom Kippur, the festival for feeling sorry and of saying sorry to people and to God. Jews pray about three things at that time: 'tzedekah' (fairness), 't'filah' (prayer) and 't'shuvah' (changing for the better). In this modern version of the story, the children's names are taken from these three things.

Zedka thought they might have all come up with the same ideas: had they, or are they all quite different ideas really? Did they need to choose one or can they have three *most* precious things? Which one might God pick, if any? What was the most precious question the children asked?

What it's worth

The sun had hardly risen and already it was stronger than anyone could bear. For months there had been no rain and the land was dry, their water cisterns were dry, and their throats were dry. If nothing happened soon, maybe even their hope would dry out.

The crops had long since been eaten and nothing would grow in the cracked soil of Medina, the city so loved by the Prophet Muhammad – the first home of the Muslim community.

Before the famine, Medina was an oasis in the desert, a fresh and vibrant spot in a stretch of scorching sand as far as the eye could see.

Now shops were shut, stalls folded away and merchants long gone. The town that had once been bustling and noisy was deserted and eerie, and the only sounds to be heard were the stirring calls to prayer five times a day and the pitiful cries of starving babies.

For a while, wealthy families still had water from their private wells and had laid in stocks of food, but they too ran out. Lounging under the shade of palm trees, they could only dream they were sipping cool drinks, sucking slices of juicy melon and chewing dates.

From beneath a canopy on the flat roof of her home, Laila's eye caught something tiny shimmering on the horizon. She leapt up in excitement, pointing and shrieking, 'Look!'

They *did* look but saw nothing.

'It's a mirage, stupid!' sneered Laila's brother. But she was right...making its way over the sand dunes was the heavily laden camel caravan of Utman, the third calif, a rich and well-respected businessman who had been on a shopping expedition.

'We are saved!' shouted Laila's thrilled parents, and by the time they had reached the gates of the city, the whole neighbourhood had heard of Laila's sighting and were following close behind. Some even ran out through the gates and over the burning hot sand to meet Utman.

'What did you get?' they clamoured to know, tugging at his kaftan and almost pulling him off his camel.

'I'll take the lot!' pressed one of the richest men in Medina.

'No way!' replied Utman, with a wave of the hand.

'I'll double the offer!' shouted another.

'No chance!'

'We'll pay you *three* times what it cost you!' bid the sisters who dealt in spices.

'No. Sorry!' responded Utman, with a perplexed smile.

'I can raise that to four!' proclaimed a metalsmith, pushing his way to the front of the crowd.

'Nothing doing, I'm afraid!' Utman insisted.

'Five!'

'Not interested!'

About 1400 year ago, when the Prophet Muhammad died, four califs – one after the other – became leader of the Muslim community. Muslims have kept alive the stories of the califs and their example of good living.

'I'll go up to six times what the load is worth!' said the silk trader. 'How would you like it? Cloth? perfume? gems? gold?'

'Madam, I don't care how you pay because you are *not* paying,' Utman explained firmly.

'Now here's an offer you can't refuse!' boasted a jeweller, weighing words carefully. 'Seven, S–E–V–E–N times what you paid, cash in hand!'

By now, with crowds pressing all around, Utman had reached the archway into Medina and dismounted. 'Look, you can make me offers until the camels come home, but this food is not for sale simply because it belongs to someone else who is paying me *ten times* what it's worth.'

'Ten?' they gasped.

'You heard! Now would you please let me pass?'

There was a stunned silence. Whoever could that be? The only way to find out was to follow Utman. They caught up with him and tagged along behind as he headed for downtown Medina where he unloaded his camel bags onto the streets.

'Allah is great!' he called. 'Come to eat!' and he handed out armfuls of food to the poor. It was beyond their wildest dreams and Utman saw sad faces changed by looks of surprise, smiles of thankfulness and tears of joy.

What made Utman refuse the wonderful offers for his goods? Did you have any idea of the 'someone' who had already bought it all? Had it really all been bought?

In what ways would Utman get paid by Allah ten times over? Do people usually get rewarded for the good things they do?

'Liar! Cheat!' shouted the wealthy mob behind him with angry eyes and clenched fists. 'No one bought it for ten times more! You deserve to be . . .!'

'*Allah* is the someone!' Utman explained. 'Look at the difference it's made to these beloved people. Don't you remember that it says in our Holy Qur'an that if you do something good, Allah will reward that ten times over.'

In the distance, the muezzin was calling from the minar at the set time: '. . . Come to prayer! Come to success!'

Something in the air

The moment Mishka opened her eyes, she knew there was something wrong. Her pillow was slimy to the touch, making her flesh creep, and the air seemed foggy and dank. Half hoping she was just dreaming, she stretched her arms and yawned – it made her tongue go sticky and warts appeared on her lips. 'Ugh!' She sniffed the air but her nostrils and throat seized up and a sharp pain gripped her chest. Her head started spinning and she felt sick in the pit of her stomach.

Sobbing only made her head hurt more and she began wondering if there was something drilling or banging inside her brain. 'I'm not staying here!' Still dizzy, she staggered across the room to the window: there was a swirling mist so thick and steamy that she could barely see the rest of Vrindavan, though across the street she could hear people bustling about and calling to each other. In the distance, the waters of the Yamuna were turbulent.

Downstairs, Mishka's parents were in a state of distress. 'It's coming up from the river, enveloping everything. We're practically suffocating,' they wailed. But Mishka just wanted to know why!

'There she goes again, asking questions!' her mother complained. 'Some things you're better off *not* knowing!'

'I *do* want to know everything,' thought Mishka. 'They treat me like a baby! And I have a *right* to know what keeps sending up these wafts of putrid air . . .' and she stormed out.

Everyone else in the village seemed to be spluttering and

scratching. Women's saris were discoloured and whitewashed houses were stained by the smog. There were babies with weeping sores and children with streaming eyes. Adults had swollen joints and the elderly had blistered skin.

Mishka decided she would keep her eyes and ears open, and gradually she was able to piece together part of the story. It seemed that a serpent had swum into the river Yamuna, just where it widens out to form a lake. He was so vile that he even contaminated the air and birds flying overhead were overcome by the fumes and crashed into the torrent. Kaliya had more heads and tails than anyone could count and when he thrashed about, he created such a commotion that the land around the Yamuna was drenched and nothing could stay alive – trees, crops, animals, even people...

Terror struck the villagers' hearts as agitated voices came from the field between Vrindavan and the river. Was Kaliya coming to attack? Surely he could not survive out of the water.

Panting and gasping, some cowherds were racing towards the anxious, huddled crowds...but they were beaming. 'As we were tending our cows, we noticed the unmistakeable footprints of Krishna. He has come to us...'

'All thanks and praise to Lord Krishna!' uttered an ecstatic old woman. 'He will always rescue those who are devoted to him and drive away all evil from their life!'

Passing through the fields with the others, Mishka saw clearly enough the special marks of Krishna's feet – a flag, a bow, a shell – but they also met his mother, Yashoda, in tears. Nanda was trying to comfort his wife but he, too, was overcome with worry and grief and their other son, Balarama,

stood by helplessly. 'We can tell he's in danger,' wept Yashoda. 'Where is he? What's he doing!'

They might have known. . . Krishna had already climbed a kadamba tree – the only one that had not withered on the riverbank – and its tiny, round, yellow flowers framed his face, making him look even younger than he was.

The spectators gasped when Krishna suddently leapt and plunged into the water. He flapped his arms, kicked his legs and created such a splash that the Yamuna flooded its banks. Frolicking in the water, Krishna looked like a playful little elephant enjoying a cool dip but Kaliya soon sensed that a force had invaded his territory. His many heads rose up above the water and with each cruel, ugly mouth he spat and hissed. Writhing about and thwacking the surface of the river with his tails, he created a terrifying thud. Then he lunged forward, grabbed Krishna with his powerful coils and gripped him tight.

The earth began to tremble, meteors crashed through the sky and shivers ran down everyone's spine.

Instinctively, Yashoda rushed to protect her child and Nanda and Balarama had to pull her back, afraid she would swallow some poison.

Mishka loved Krishna so much that she felt she, too, was struggling with evil. She thought about all the creepy things she had ever done – or just thought – and was filled with shame. She was sorry she had had horrid thoughts about her Ba and Baba at home earlier. 'Why did I have to be so nasty? If Krishna can get rid of Kaliya,' she decided, 'I can get rid of all the nasty things in me.' For two hours it went on, Krishna in the clutches of Kaliya and Mishka in the clutches of her own guilt. Then, suddenly she felt an elbow nudging her. 'Look!'

A different kind of power was coursing through Krishna. His body started to expand so much that Kaliya's strength was stretched to the limit. He strained to hold the baby Lord but he could not: the coils slackened, his stranglehold was released and Krishna slipped from his grasp.

Unconquered and with his eyes blazing in fury, Kaliya spread out his hoods, blew poison from his mouths and exhaled fire from his nostrils. Then it was Krishna's turn to act. Bouncing from one head to another, he stunned and confused the wicked monster who spat out wildly but missed every time. Krishna pounced again. Once more the creature emitted a noxious substance and once more his opponent with nimble feet outwitted him. Higher and higher Krishna leapt until he was dancing on the tallest hood. In a last attempt to defeat his destroyer, the enraged serpent thrust at him with all his vicious heads at once but Krishna was just out of reach. Exhausted, the multi-headed snake finally surrendered and slumped into the water.

Still hopping sprightly on Kaliya's highest head, Krishna took out his flute and, with his face all aglow, he played the sweetest tune the exultant villagers had ever heard. Humiliated, Kaliya slunk down the river and out of sight.

At once, the water became clear and blue, and fish swam about freely. Grass turned lush and green, and trees blossomed again. 'Evil has gone! God is good!' shouted the people. Lord Krishna touched dry land, his worshippers garlanded him with flowers and spread petals at his feet.

'Mishka? Mishka?' a frantic mother was calling. Mishka would have known that voice anywhere.

'I'm here, Ba! What's the matter?'

'Oh, thank goodness you're all right...' panted her mother, pushing through the crowds. 'I've been so worried about you all day. You just went off without saying where you were going and I was afraid maybe you'd, you know...'

'Oh, Ba!' said Mishka, stroking her mother's cheek. 'I'm...'

'What, Mishka?' she asked softly.

'Oh nothing, Ba,' she replied and gave her a little squeeze. 'It's all right!'

Hindus believe that God appears in life in many different ways. As Vishnu, who preserves the world, he can take the form of Krishna and many Hindus worship Krishna as God. There is a tradition of stories in which Krishna likes playing and is small but strong.

Do we all have bad things inside us that we feel ashamed of? How did they get there? Can we get rid of them by ourselves? How? Does it help to have stories of God removing evil from the world? If we are unhappy or unwell, does it help to know *why*? Do we have a right to know *everything*?

All together

A wedding was the last thing in the world on Ms Hind's mind. Everyone told her it was time she settled down, but she didn't fancy the idea at all. It wasn't the actual ceremony she minded. In fact, she liked being the centre of attraction and she hadn't been to a decent party for ages. What really bothered her was the idea of being tied down and not being able to do what she wanted. She had her career to think of.

'If you met the right man,' her mother said softly, 'someone who'd make a fuss of you and let you have a bit of your own life, you wouldn't feel like that. Perhaps you could do things together. Your father and I only want you to be happy... There are so many really nice young men interested in you but you never give them a chance.'

'Oh, Mummy, they're such creeps!'

'Not all of them, dear. Why don't you let us arrange something?'

'All right – but only if I can choose.'

'Of course, darling.'

Mr and Mrs Hind worked really fast and lined up six eligible bachelors for her to meet. Their daughter had been working fast too and had devised a clever plan to find out which guy – if any – was the man for her. She got the idea from a party game she played when she was about ten: everyone is blindfolded and they have to guess what something is by feeling it.

Getting hold of an elephant for a day wasn't exactly easy but well worth the effort. She led it into the yard and gave it plenty to eat so it wouldn't be noisy and give the game away.

'Is this their idea of "Mr Wonderful"?' Ms Hind thought when she saw her admirers. They all agreed to the test.

'Too tight?' she asked as she blindfolded the first one.

'It's fine, my sweet.'

'My sweet!' she thought. 'Yuk!' And she led him into the yard to identify the mystery object.

'I hope you're not peeping!' she said to the second one.

'You *know* I only have eyes for you!'

'Good grief!' she muttered. 'This way, please.'

'Ouch! you're hurting me!' screamed the third, but she tugged the wimp by the arm and led him into the yard with the others.

'What kind of knot are you using?' the fourth suitor enquired.

'A strong one!' retorted Ms Hind, thinking to herself, 'what a wally!'

The fifth in line stood with his arms by his side and let her apply the blindfold but she never respected anyone who seemed weak.

By the time it was the turn of the sixth, and tallest, there was no pleasing her at all.

The six rivals staggered about in the yard, their arms stretched out in front of them, and finally each one caught hold of one part of the elephant's body.

This story probably once came from India though it has been told in many countries with slightly different details. It is a good example of the way stories change by being told over and over again.

Usually, the characters are *actually* blind and it is a king who gives them the puzzle to solve about how we see life. Quite a lot of Hindu folktales have parents looking for a suitable 'match' for their daughter or son. This modern version combines the two kinds of stories but with a slight twist: the young woman wants to take her pick...

'Well, what is it?' Ms Hind called from the balcony.

The first one was holding the trunk. 'It's a pipe, my sweet!'

'Wrong – *my sweet!*' she snapped.

Nearby, the second called out, 'It's a spear!' He was gripping the animal's tusk.

'No!'

'I'm sure it's a tree,' the third chipped in. He had wrapped his arms round one of the legs.

'Nothing like!' she shouted. Three down – three to go!

From the tail end, the fourth in the guessing-game yelled, 'A rope!'

'Wrong as well!'

All this time, the fifth contestant had been stroking the huge creature's side.

'It's definitely a wall!'

'It's definitely not!'

Finally, the tall man had stretched to the elephant's ear. 'With this, my love, I shall fan you on hot days!'

'I'm cool already!' she rebuffed.

What might have happened if the six young men *had* shared what they felt? Would they have worked out that it was an elephant? If they did, what would be *Ms Hind's* problem then? How could the story go on from there?

Why had the elephant vanished when they took off their blindfolds? Was it *ever* there at all? What could the elephant represent?

'You have *all* missed the point. You can't break anything into bits and expect to know what it's really like. It isn't even all the bits added up. You have to see it as a whole. If you'd only talked to each other and shared what you knew, you could have worked it out. Nobody ever has all the answers and sometimes we think we see things that aren't even there. So, you're dying to know what it is? It is an elephant. Take off your blindfolds and see for yourself.'

But when they turned round to look...the elephant had vanished.

Cup final

Miri and Jess stared at each other in amazement, pinched themselves to make sure they were not dreaming and read the telegram again.

JESSE AND MIRIAM STONE
7 VESSEL GARDENS   GLASTONBURY
CONGRATULATIONS ON WINNING ENTRY IN FOOTBALL COMPETITION STOP ALL FIVE QUESTIONS ANSWERED CORRECTLY AND SPOT THE BALL MOST ACCURATE EVER RECORDED STOP FIRST PRIZE MYSTERY TOUR IN SPECIALLY DESIGNED VEHICLE 'TEMPLE OF QUEST' STOP VISIT SEVEN MAJOR WORLD CENTRES STOP STAR PRIZE IF LOCATE HIDDEN CUP OR BOWL AND ASK RIGHT QUESTION TO UNLOCK SECRET STOP MUST BE READY TO START NOW

It was the most exciting thing that had ever happened to the twins and they could hardly believe their good luck. They had always wanted the chance to see the world and the 'Temple of Quest' sounded intriguing. Perhaps it will be like one of those time-ships in science fiction programmes, they wondered. Yet they were puzzled by the extra challenge they had been set: something which looked like a cup or a bowl. 'That could be anything,' Miri remarked. 'But maybe the Temple of Quest will take us to it,' she added, trying to be helpful. 'And anyway, if they blot the football out of the photo of a match and we managed to guess where it would have been, surely we can find a glass or a dish! I'm much more bothered by the questions we have to ask: I don't normally go around quizzing coffee mugs or washing-up bowls!'

The Temple of Quest turned out to be a ball of smoky glass which bounced along Vessel Gardens. It had nothing inside but above the number five flashed all the time until it landed and Jess thought they had gone around the corner.

There were not, in fact, in Glastonbury but outside a church in Guatemala. In front was a huge crucifix, bearing the carved figure of Christ dying. They could hear singing and a guitar being played in the church. Underneath a brightly coloured painting of Jesus feeding the five thousand with only five small loaves, the priest was celebrating Mass on the altar. 'This is my blood which is shed for you...' he proclaimed and in both hands he held high a silver goblet. They wondered if that was *the* cup but had to wait until the Mass had ended to find out.

'The Mass is a mystery – we feel it – it's hard to understand,' the priest explained, 'but Jesus *did* know he was going to die and at a special dinner with his best friends, he picked up his wine glass and said, "I'm pouring out my blood for you!" We say that at the Mass.' He must have known what Miri and Jess were thinking because he went on, 'We put *wine* in the cup – not blood – but we believe that the spirit of the wine changes into the spirit of Christ's blood. Some people say Jesus' cup was used to collect drops of his actual blood and then put in a secret place... You would like to find Jesus' *actual* cup?' The priest smiled, laid his hands on their heads and continued, 'The chalice we use in the Mass is simply the same shape as the cup from which Jesus drank and into which his blood dripped. His cup was full of suffering. To understand that, you have to go out into the world. Unless you do, you won't find the mystery in here.'

'Then what is your church for?' Miri asked.

'God bless you, children!'

By now, the Temple of Quest was bobbing up and down in the town square and they climbed in. It was another short trip. . .and they had to stoop a little not to bump into the strings of brightly coloured lanterns which looked enchanting against the twilight sky. 'Welcome to "The Good Luck Garden"!' said the old man and he pointed to some cushions by a low table. As he poured them steaming tea from a blue and white porcelain teapot decorated with dragons, he noticed Jess staring, and Jess noticed that he noticed! Embarrassed, Jess mused, 'I notice there aren't many leaves in this kind of tea!'

'I don't need leaves: I'm not a fortune teller,' the old man joked. 'There is no magic in this tea, though it is made according to an ancient Chinese recipe – simple but secret – using herbs, to promote long life and well being. I drink five cups a day and have great mental powers and inner calm.'

'How do you find peace of mind?' Jess wanted to know.

'Be happy in your search!' was the reply.

'Back to the bubble!' piped Miri. 'We blew that one, too! But the next place I've seen on TV – they have baseball here!'

'Doesn't look like a sports stadium to me. More like an outdoor music hall,' Jess replied but just then the clown act finished, the audience exploded with laughter and applause and the announcer came back onto the stage. 'And now, ladies and gentlemen, will you welcome back to the Hollywood Bowl our stars for tonight, "The Bunch of Five"! Yeah!' Shrieks, whistles and loud clapping brought the quintuplets on and the band struck up. 'Just look at those costumes and face paint!' exclaimed Jess. 'They're more made up than the clowns!'

'What's it all about?' they sang as a neon sign flashed 'The Real Thing' against a starless sky.

'What *is* real?' asked Jess as they got up to go.

'Have a nice day!' said a voice behind them.

The sky was bright with stars when they arrived at an African village. Outside a woman was grinding corn in a stone mill.

Inside, her five children lay sleeping. Miri offered to help but the woman replied, 'No, my child it has a rhythm, and I am used to this work. The drought killed all the families but ours – and today...' she paused and looked down. 'Today, my husband died. This is all the corn I have now. In the morning I will cook sudsa and we will eat our last meal.'

The twins were quiet for a while, listening to the slow, even grinding and seeing the faith in the woman's eyes. 'What do you need to live?' Miri asked, with tears on her cheeks.

'We have a saying, "Every child brings its own bread".'

'We can't leave them to die, Miri...but you know she'd never come...'

The Soviet surgeon was proud to show the young travellers the new hospital. Above the operating table was a large mirror. 'This enables us to see the whole body without stretching over the patient,' she explained. The patient was drinking from a clear perspex cup. 'That's the pre-med, before the full anaesthetic. This man's body is riddled with cancer which we shall remove but it's very far gone as he didn't go to his doctor when he first felt unwell five years ago. If only he had...modern medicine is marvellous...'

'Are we only a body, then?' Jess wondered.

'I'm afraid you must leave as the operation is starting.'

The Temple of Quest looked strange outside the angular concrete building. 'Off we go, comrade!'

'Isn't that lovely, sis?' shouted Jess, running towards the fountain to catch its spray. 'The sun has cast a rainbow over it – look! Let's throw three coins in the fountain and make our wish! And no telling!'

'We've still got two coins left – what about an icecream each?' Miri begged. 'One Paradiso and one Perfetto, please!'

They sat in the sunshine, on the the edge of the fountain bowl, madly trying to lick the icecream before it totally melted. 'Is there anything that lasts?' Miri asked.

'Arriverderci, Roma!' the icecream seller called.

'Have you noticed how no one ever answers our questions, Miri?'

'Jess, where on earth are we now? We could be anywhere and there's no one in sight...'

The Temple of Quest hovered over a circle of five hills which surrounded a deep crater. They could make out the ruins of buildings and vehicles, and the remains of a bridge.

'I think a bomb's been dropped...that's why there's no sign of life...don't go any further...'

'I'm scared, Miri!'

'Hug me, Jess!'

Without speaking, they knew deep inside them that they must not look up. If they did, they would surely see the mushroom cloud – not the cup-shape they were seeking, but the cup-shape they were dreading... They flung their arms around each other's necks... 'Is this the end?'

There are many legends about the Grail, the cup from which Jesus drank and in which drops of his blood were collected. About 1000 years go, there was a belief that if someone found the cup, asked it the right question and drank water from it, all the mysteries of life would be shown to them and they would live for ever. The Grail came in many forms and was sometimes even a stone: some thought about Jesus when they were searching for it and some thought of Mary. Often there would be a light or some sign above the Grail and the number five would somehow be important. This is an adventure based on the Grail legends, with questions that young people might ask today.

Nobody ever answered the twins' questions but did they get answers in other ways?
What question would you like to ask?

Published by BBC Books and Longman Group UK Limited

BBC Books
a division of
BBC Enterprises Limited
Woodlands
80 Wood Lane
London W12 0TT

Longman Group UK Limited.
Longman House,
Burnt Mill,
Harlow,
Essex,
CM20 2JE,
England and Associated
Companies throughout
the World.

First published 1990
Fourth impression 1995

Illustrations by **Avril Turner**, **John Blackman** and **Norman Young**
Cover illustration by **John Blackman**
Cover and book design by **Alix Harrower**

ISBN 0 582 05946 1

Set in Gill Sans and Stempel Garamond
Produced by Longman Singapore Publishers Pte Ltd
Printed in Singapore

The Publisher's policy is to use paper manufactured from sustainable forests.